BREAKIN' OUT OF YOUR FINANCIAL FUNK!

Ida Byrd-Hill

A Practical Guide to
Personal and Financial Success

Upheaval Media, Inc.

© 2008 by Ida Byrd-Hill. All rights reserved.

ISBN: 978-0-6151-9321-2

Library of Congress Control Number: 2008924038

All rights reserved. No part of this book may be used or reproduced in any manner whatsoever without the written permission of the Author. Printed in the United States of America. For information address: Ida Byrd-Hill, Uplift Inc., P.O. Box 241488, Detroit, MI 48224

Book design by Louise Pastula with Color Montage
www.colormontage.com

I dedicate this book to God
who has given me the ability to create ideas;
my children who inspire me to innovate
and my parents who instilled strong values.

INTRODUCTION 1
FINANCIAL FUNK DEFINED 2
   Affluent Financial Funk
   Common Financial Funk
   Financial Funk Quiz
   Emotions of Financial Funk
   Fear of Failure
   The Past - The Key to the Present
   Fear of Success
LACK OF SELF CONFIDENCE 12
   CONFIDENCE QUIZ
HOW TO DEVELOP YOUR SELF-CONFIDENCE 21
DREAMS 25
   Dream, if you dare!
   As a Man Thinketh
   Passionate dreams
LIFESTYLE OPTIONS 34
   Lifestyle exactly the same
   Pursue a Hobby in New Job/Career
   New Job in the Same Career
   TURN YOUR HOBBY INTO A BUSINESS!!
   Analyze Yourself
   Volunteer Work
DREAMING IS ABOUT REALITY 45
   How to Attract Money
   Six steps to Dream Programming:
   What is your belief?
   101 Goals
APPENDIX 63
   ABOUT THE AUTHOR
   Speaking Inquiry
   Share your Stories

INTRODUCTION

The last few years have been difficult years for all Americans. We attempted to recover from the collapse of the World Trade Center that occurred in September 2001 only to be terrorized by the war in Iraq. Our country besieged by the recession endured by massive layoffs, significant pay cuts and bonus eliminations. People saw the stock market whittle their life savings or estates to less than half. Others endured home foreclosures and personal bankruptcies. Some have watched major businesses liquidate while others saw their business revenues dissipate.

Still others are living well just not as well, because they have had to reduce some of their luxuries. Yes, they are still traveling worldwide, just not as frequent. Yes, they are buying expensive clothes. For the first time discount shopping has become the new rage even amongst the super wealthy. Everyone is bragging about the sales they have taken advantaged of. Yes, they are buying fancy cars, but now they are looking for a deal too. There were parties everywhere this year end as people were attempting to drown the pain, but these parties were less elaborate than they were in the past.

No matter how wealthy or poor, we are feeling the bad mood - **The FUNK-** the last two years have created. The playing field has been leveled as all Americans have modified their lives somewhat. We can all feel the pain of being in a Financial Funk. The question is "how do we get out of this Financial Funk?"

This book, **Breakin' Out of Your Financial Funk**, attempts to show people at every level, upper-class, middle-class, lower-class, how to break out of the financial funk they are experiencing. This book combines theoretical knowledge that the author, Ida Byrd-Hill, has gained as a financial planner and practical experience she garnered while **Breakin' out of her financial funk.**

Chapter 1

FINANCIAL FUNK DEFINED

For eight years, I owned a successful financial services firm that I built from the ground floor. We had gained a significant share of wealthy clients. Our office was furnished with rich, cherry wood furniture and overlooked the Detroit River. We had money in the bank. We lived a jet-set life, traveling all over the world. We were pampered by a foreign housekeeper, nanny, landscaper and personal assistants. However, in the ninth year the bottom fell out. My revenues decreased sharply. I blamed the decrease on the recession. That was partly true. The truth was I wanted to do something else. I wanted to build houses, schools, recreation facilities and write a book. I did not want to disturb my life. As I spent my savings, I was in a Financial Funk.

A Financial Funk is a bad mood reflected in one's finances. Everyone faces obstacles along the path of life to success. However, when those obstacles create a path themselves or the obstacles weigh down your subconscious causing you to perform acts that reduce or strip you finances, you are now in a bad mood financially. Financial funk is not just suffering financially, it is suffering mentally which affects your finances. It took me a year to realize I was in a financial funk, as my lifestyle remained primarily the same. Then the financial bottom fell out. In 2004, I decided to leave the financial advisory field to pursue my new dreams. Despite the pain of laying off my housekeeper, nanny, landscaper and two personal assistants, I was determined to come out of this financial funk. Well, as you can see Financial Funk can occur in many facets. Let us look at the two extremes of financial funk: the affluent and the commoner.

Affluent Financial Funk

The American Dream is to be a happily married couple, living in a 3000 to 5000 square foot home in an affluent neighborhood, decorated by a professional interior designer wearing the latest fashions purchased at Bloomingdale's, Saks Fifth Avenue or Neiman's. Your children attend a prestigious private or public school. You belong to the prominent country clubs, yacht clubs and social clubs. You, even, vacation amongst the wealthy at exotic locations around the world. Everyone knows and respect you. So many young professionals want to be like you.

Consider how your normal workday proceeds: *Alarm buzzes at 5:30 am. We slowly arise, as we stumble to the gym to workout and then shower. It takes us 1 hour to dry and style our hair. Get dressed; wake up the children and get them dressed. Darn the nanny is late again!!! We need to find time to hire a live-in nanny. Prepare breakfast to be eaten now or maybe in the car on the run. Drop the kids off at day care or school. Jump on the highway for the grueling drive (or should I say parking lot) to work. Get to work and deal with demanding clients and get undermined politically by your boss, as you want to scream but you smile while containing your anger. The clock chimes 5:00 p.m., work still not done so you work until 7:00 p.m. when you have to attend a social function. A major client is in town. You socialize well and you even convince the client to purchase more of your services. Back into the car, arrive at home, vegetated by the rush home only to find you children are asleep and you have not seen them another evening. Once home, you listen to your spouse's story. They are boring. You go to the den, light the fireplace and mix up apple martinis at your mahogany bar as your spouse lectures you on the necessity of you visiting the kids at least once during the week. You*

Chapter 1

sit looking out at stars through your expensive sun roof. You gaze excitedly as you spent a few thousand for this modern convenience and you can finally enjoy it. You finally retire to the bedroom exhausted only to prepare for another day, to make another dollar....

This scene repeats itself 5 days in a row then the weekend comes. The weekend comes...

The same children who drag out of bed Monday thru Friday wake up instantly at 7:00 a.m. to watch cartoons. You finally see them. You decide to make breakfast; it burns and smokes up the house. You rush to the local pancake house that is packed to the maximum. Than return home from eating a nice family breakfast, finally relax in your leather designer easy chair and hear: "What's for lunch?" The kids want sushi. Your spouse decides he wants potato chips. So you fly back to the store for soda, sushi and potato chips. The kids want to play outside, therefore, you go outside to watch over them. The landscaping looks mediocre so you call the landscaper who decides to charge you extra for Saturday services. It's 7:00 p.m. and you need to dress for social party. You realize the housekeeper did not pick up your tuxedo or evening gown. You dash to the closest Saks' to get a new tuxedo/evening gown. Late again! You arrive at the party and the usual movers and shakers are there. You try to party hardy!!! People are so sophisticated; so sophisticated, they are really boring.

Get home. Ready to go to bed. What a weekend......

Our lives continue to spiral these scenes over and over again. Before we know it, years have whizzed by and we ask ourselves: *"What have we accomplished?"*

Financial Funk Defined

We have accomplished: "depression, stress and anxiety" as stated by 60 percent of the sample group of Douglas LaBier's book **_Modern Madness_**. We have developed high blood pressure, heart attacks and strokes at earlier ages. Even though more and more Americans have reached the success level of money, power and position we have lost ourselves and our lives of personal fulfillment and meaning. Although we are making more money than ever, our savings rate as Americans has dropped to 4.5% in 1995 from a high of 8.6% in 1973. *(The Japanese save 15%)* while our consumer debt has escalated to 984 billion, or approximately $3500 per child, man or woman.

***"Debt is one of our main shackles. Our levels of debt and our lack of savings make the nine-to-five routine mandatory. Between our mortgages, car financing and credit card debts, we can not afford to quit any job,"* even if it makes us sick**.

The very essence of our lives is sucked from us as we begrudgingly occupy a job/career/lifestyle that now bores or depresses us. What can we do? Vicariously, we hold these trappings near and dear to our hearts. Society even praises us for acquiring these trappings. These social circles define our external lives. Do we attempt to maintain the American Dream quota even though it is killing us? We are in a financial funk as we are on a treadmill and can not get off. We pat ourselves on the back that we are not living the life, those people, the commoners, are living.

Chapter 1

Common Financial Funk

Consider how our normal work day proceeds: *Alarm buzzes at 5:00 am. We slowly arise, as we stumble to the shower. Then we have to dry and style our hair. We get dressed; wake up the children and get them dressed. Prepare breakfast to be eaten now or maybe in the car on the run. Drop the kids off at day care or school. Jump on the highway for the grueling drive (or should I say parking lot) to work only to get to work and deal with your demanding boss. Your boss cuts your pay. You want to scream but you smile while containing your anger as you "need "this job. The school calls because your son is misbehaving. You stop what you are doing and go to the school. The gnawing pain of hunger causes you to get a headache because you missed lunch again. The clock chimes 5:00 p.m. and your work is still not done, but you must pick up kids by 6:00 p.m. to escape the horrendous late fees of childcare. Back into the car, you arrive home vegetated by the rush home, only to go to home and work another eight hours. Once home, you must listen to the children's school stories, interrupted occasionally by bill collectors, then listen to your spouse's story. You cook dinner, clean the kitchen and then interact as a family, in front of the boob tube or help the children do homework. Your spouse gets drunk and you fight for an hour. You forgot the repo-man is looking to pick up your car so you jump back into the car and hide it in your neighbor's garage around the corner. Exhausted by today's happenings you finally retire to the bedroom to prepare for another day, to make another dollar or shall I say another quarter....*

This scene repeats itself 5 days in a row, then the weekend comes...

Financial Funk Defined

The same children that you drag out of bed Monday thru Friday wake up instantly at 7:00 a.m. to watch cartoons. You must get up to make breakfast. Then you start cleaning the house since you had no time to do it during the week. You get the kids ready for the day. Hurry to wash your hair and shower; only to chauffeur the kids from activity to activity. Rush to the grocery store on Saturday to beat the Sunday madness. Rush to dry cleaners before it closes. Come home and relax in your easy chair; but how can you relax when that stack of bills is staring you in the face. You get up and balance your checkbook. Whew!!! Not enough to pay the bills again. The children ask: "What's for dinner?", so you get up to cook dinner and realize nothing available for an easy dinner. You call the nearest pizza for delivery and your spouse wants soda. So your rush back to the store for soda, cookies and potato chips. The kids want to play outside so you go outside to watch over them. You notice that the landscaping needs some work so you cut grass, and attempt to trim the bushes. You need new hedge trimmers. You visit the hardware store to get new hedge trimmers and come home with nails and drywall for a new project to build a basement office. OOP's forgot hedge trimmers. Its 6:30 p.m.; you were invited to a social party. You pass, too exhausted to party. You watch the boob tube until you fall asleep on the sofa, again.

What a weekend…..

Chapter 1

If you are still not sure you are in a financial funk, Take this Financial Funk Quiz.
(5 points for each C answer, 3 points for each B answer, 1 point for each A answer.)

Financial Funk Quiz

1. Your alarm clock on buzzes at 5:30 am. Do you? ___
    a) Jump out of bed excited to face the day.
    b) Slowly get out of bed, shower, dress arriving 10-20 minutes late.
    c) Continually hit the snooze button until it is 7:00 a.m. knowing you are 40 minutes from your job which begins at 8:00 am.

2. Your average workday: _____
    a) Flies by with you enjoying every minute.
    b) Crawls at a snail's pace.
    c) Is just that—another day.

3. Your work: _____
    a) Excites you to the point of becoming a workaholic.
    b) Bore you to death.
    c) Leaves you drained at the end of the day.

4. My job/my business: _____
    a) Is my dream.
    b) Allows me to obtain the finer things in life.
    c) Is the means to a paycheck.

5. My career/ my business: _____
    a) Is growing upwardly by leaps and bounds.
    b) Grows laterally as I pick up different skills.
    c) Has remained the same.

Financial Funk Defined

6. When you arrive at home you: _____
   a) Play with the kids enthusiastically.
   b) Eat dinner and go to sleep.
   c) Yell at the kids.

7. Your stresses causes you to: _____
   a) Exercise for relief.
   b) Drink alcohol to relieve yourself.
   c) Beat your wife and kids.

8. You are addicted to: _____
   a) Alcohol, drugs, prescription.
   b) Food, sex, shopping.
   c) Beat your wife and kids.

9. You are: _____
   a) Calm and peaceful.
   b) Bored.
   c) Frustrated.

10. Your greatest complaint is: _____
    a) "I need more social time."
    b) "I have too many bills."
    c) "I lack money."

Chapter 1

Score

50-36 Points

You are in a **FINANCIAL FUNK**. Your finances are decreasing or your lifestyle drains you as it is not what you desire. You need to discover who you really are and what passion drives you. You can solve your financial woes by identifying skills that you have that are transferable to a new passionate career/ business or second job.

35-25 Points

You are on the Verge of **FINANCIAL FUNK**. Your lifestyle may excite you but other external circumstances frustrate you. You need to discover if you truly love your current passion and how to rid yourself of the frustrations that are weighing you down. You also need to seek that passion actively rather than activities to hide your pain.

24 - Below Points

Congratulations! You are living a **DREAM** life. Your lifestyle excites you and your finances are in order. You need to know what a **FINANCIAL FUNK** looks like, so you may never experience it.

Financial Funk Defined

Living in the world of capitalism, it is easy to fall into a financial funk. We are not judged by our personalities alone; but rather we receive social status by the things we own, the jobs we hold, the income we generate, and the cash we accumulate. Your social status is determined by two things: cash accumulation or good credit. If you lose your good credit, you can use cash to restore it. Lose your cash and you will soon lose your good credit. With that loss, you will be relegated to second class citizenship, where you get poor services and poor treatment. Most people can lose things but the poor treatment warps their self- esteem. We would avoid it at all cost. Our financial funk is not just the loss of money and things, it is the bad mood created by the poor treatment we receive as our circumstances changes.

Although it is easy to fall into a financial funk, it is seemingly impossible to get out. This seemingly fortress-financial funk depresses most people causing them to fall deeper into their financial funk. In order to break out of this financial funk, you must FIGHT BACK!!!!! Let's not fight with the family, but let's fight the issues that caused you to fall into your financial funk: Your Emotional State, Lack of Cash and Excessive Debt!

Chapter 2

EMOTIONS OF FINANCIAL FUNK

You may be asking yourself how did I get in this FINANCIAL FUNK??? It is pure and simple. The human mind responds to these stimulations:

1. Sexual desire-passion
2. Love
3. Burning desire for fame, power or financial gain
4. Music
5. Friendship – same sex or opposite sex
6. Harmony amongst two or more people who ally themselves for spiritual or temporal advancement
7. Mutual suffering
8. Autosuggestion
9. Fear
10. Narcotics and alcohol

Financial funk is a symptom of FEAR !!!!!

Fear of Failure

Many of us are paralyzed by the fear of failure or better yet society's perception of our failure. To sell your house in an affluent neighborhood for a simpler house in a less exclusive neighborhood is failure to most. Closing a business and opening another is failure. Many people stay locked into their lives due to fear.

Fear of failure causes people to "shop-till-they-drop", take drugs, drink alcohol to an excess, sleep excessively, overly indulge in food and sex. Fear is the root cause of most of our obsessions. We indulge, to drown the fear. **"Failure is only a temporary defeat—nature's way of readjusting your plan."** Accept it as so. Many people have accepted failure and then gone on to greatness.

Thomas Edison "*failed*" *10,000 times before he perfected the modern light bulb. His assistant frustrated by the many attempts, questioned Edison about their dilemma. Edison response was: "Yes, we have experimented with this thing 8,999 times, but I know there are 8,999 materials that won't work' and forged ahead. Edison had no formal education to remind him that he had failed. All he had was a dream that a fireless candle could be invented.*

"Every adversity, every failure, every headache carries with it the seed of an equivalent or greater benefit. When adversities, failures or headaches occur, success equals to or is greater than those failures that will come."

"I am stressed to the max!!! I am in a Financial FUNK!!!! What does this have to do with my financial crisis?" Everything!!!! This is not your first financial crisis. In fact, when you examine your life, I am willing to bet that each financial funk looks similar to each other. We all develop patterns and habits that repeat themselves. Unfortunately, we never realize what the patterns and habits are, so we keep repeating them. Let's look at our past, it is the key to our present.

The Past - The Key to the Present

Suppose someone asked you: "Who is the most important person you know today?" What would your response be—Bill Clinton, George Bush, Alan Greenspan, Bill Gates, Magic Johnson, Evelyn Ashford, Denzel Washington, Angeline Jolie, Ben Carson, etc.? Did you consider yourself in this list? Napoleon Hill states: "The most important person you know is the person you are." The secret of true success is found within

Chapter 2

yourself. Therefore, the greatest feat is to find one's real self and to find individuality as you find yourself, determining what is your life's passion.

People who chase their passions receive money. People who love what they do tend to immerse themselves into an activity they like which causes them to produce great results. Most people who are experiencing financial funk are experiencing a lifestyle or career they hate. Yes, you may have been laid off or your company downsized and you had no control over this event. Maybe you did. But maybe your company chose you to be laid off or downsized because they did not feel your performance was stellar. Think about it!!! Could it be true?

The journey into your past promotes various emotions: fear of discovering that you hate your lifestyle; anger at those who have hurt you in the past; revenge; enthusiasm; faith in yourself; loyalty. Whatever emotions this journey into the past provokes, allow them to flow effortlessly, but keep probing within. The past is a good indication of your present and future.

What is your greatest financial crisis? Is it one event or a series of events?

_____

_____

_____

_____

_____

What has been your best financial decision? Why?

_____

_____

_____

_____

_____

_____

_____

Fear of Success

The real truth of the matter is that many of us are not really afraid of failure. We are afraid of becoming great; greater even than we could ever imagine. Sounds hard to believe? This poem written in the book **Return to Love,** authored by Marianne Williamson, convinced me the fear of success is real. Read this poem 3 times slowly.

Our deepest fear is not that we are inadequate.
Our deepest fear is that we are powerful beyond measure.
It is our light, not our darkness that frightens us.
We ask ourselves, who am I to be brilliant, gorgeous, talented and fabulous?
Actually, who are we not to be?
You are a child of God.
Your playing small doesn't serve the world.
There's nothing enlightened about shrinking so that other people won't feel insecure around you.
We were born to make manifest the glory of God that is

Chapter 2

within us.
It's not just in some of us, it's in everyone.
And as we let our light shine, we unconsciously
Give people permission to do the same.
As we are liberated from our own fears,
Our presence automatically liberates others.

After I read this poem, I was brought to tears. Here I was afraid to be great. This poem shook me out of that mode. Are you afraid to be great? If you let your imagination run wild, how great could you become? I decided I could become the #1 Author on the Wall Street Journal and the New York Times Best Sellers list. I decided I could grow Uplift, Inc., become a manager of a chain of cyber schools and a large developer of affordable luxury styled homes. Nationwide, I decided I could become a top billed national speaker. That's how great I could become.

Let your imagination run wild! Define how great you can become:

_____

_____

_____

_____

_____

_____

_____

Lack of Self Confidence

Dreams and visions do not automatically become reality. They merely lay the foundation or a plan to create the reality. Faith is the unquestioning belief that does not require proof, it is the power to propel the plan into action. Faith gives man the boldness to act upon his dream even when the current circumstances or living situations demand that his dream is a fantasy. The amount of faith a person possesses depends upon how a person sees themselves in relationship with God and humankind. If a person "sees" them self as a failure, they have no faith to see their plan as a reality, therefore; they will not execute their plan. However if a person 'sees' them self as a success, their plan becomes a reality, so much as they will execute their plan. **For when obstacles surround or block out a clear vision of their dream, faith empowers them to persist beyond the roadblocks.** No faith and no confidence equals - no power.

Sad to say, most people in the world have no confidence in their abilities. Even those who publicly brag about their accomplishments have no confidence in their abilities. Yes, even those who have accomplished influential positions within corporate America. The greedy philosophy of the 1980's: "keeping up with the Jones" was built upon people's perception of how others viewed their worth. They easily succumbed to criticism (both positive and negative) of colleagues and relatives. Many refused to take risk, even calculated risk, in their lives and careers as they fear criticism from others saying: "That's a crazy idea!, Oh that won't work!", and deeper yet, criticism from themselves. How many times have you said to yourself: "I can't do that because....." the fear of criticism is related to one's self confidence. The lower the self-confidence, the greater the fear of criticism. The greater the self-confidence, the lower the fear of criticism.

Chapter 2

See how much Self-Confidence you possess. Answer these questions honestly in the Confidence Quiz.

CONFIDENCE QUIZ

Circle numbers 1-4 that honestly reflect your patterns
1-Almost Never 2-Occasionally 3-Frequently 4-Almost all the time

1. Do you surround yourself with positive people?
    1   2   3   4
2. Do you love your work?
    1   2   3   4
3. Do you love yourself when things go wrong?
    1   2   3   4
4. Are you your own best friend when you make a mistake or blow it?
    1   2   3   4
5. Do you matter to others?
    1   2   3   4
6. Do you acknowledge your own accomplishments?
    1   2   3   4
7. Do you enjoy learning new things?
    1   2   3   4
8. Are you healthy?
    1   2   3   4
9. Have you had any expert "image" consultations?
    1   2   3   4
10. Do you surround yourself with people you admire?
    1   2   3   4
11. Do you have a trusted friend or colleague that you can let your hair down with?
    1   2   3   4
12. Are you able to ask for something when you want it?
    1   2   3   4
13. When you are rejected, do you take it personally?
    1   2   3   4

14. Do you understand yourself when others don't?
    1   2   3   4
15. Can you laugh at yourself?
    1   2   3   4
16. Are you "on track" for you?
    1   2   3   4
17. Do others enjoy being around you?
    1   2   3   4
18. Do you forgive yourself for mistakes that you make?
    1   2   3   4
19. When you have failed at something, can you still be around others?
    1   2   3   4
20. Are you true to you?
    1   2   3   4

Add up each column _____ _____ _____ _____

Total all numbers. This is your final score: _____

SCORE

72 -80 points

BRAVO!!! You are an accomplished person who has a sense of who you are. Although you have learned how to get, keep and grow confidence, read this section to remind yourself of how you developed that confidence.

61-71 points

IMPRESSIVE!!! You have a strong sense of confidence, which is illustrated in your leadership abilities to achieve your dreams. Your sense of "self" is definitely a key ingredient to move on to be the greatest success ever. However, your confidence needs a little fine-tuning. Please read on.

Chapter 2

50-60 points

AVERAGE!!! Your confidence level is average, meaning you will yield an average return in achieving your dream. Perhaps it is time for you to stretch yourself - to learn something new about yourself and your chosen career passion. Read on to find out how to transform your current career to a new found passion.

39-49 points

SHAKY!!! Your confidence level waivers -- one moment you feel you can conquer the world – the next moment you feel you can't do anything right. Let's stabilize your confidence. Read on.

Below 38

YIKES!!! Major confidence surgery is needed. You seek negative people and situations to confirm your low self-confidence. Read on to quickly repair your confidence; as "no one can make you feel inferior without your permission" *Eleanor Roosevelt*

Before you can tackle your creditors, make lifestyle adjustments and break out of your Financial Funk, you must possess the self-confidence that your financial funk is not the end of the world and that you can break out of it.

HOW TO DEVELOP YOUR SELF-CONFIDENCE

The word SELF-CONFIDENCE is defined as a certainty or belief in your abilities and your image of what you are worth within society-at-large. Whew! What a definition! Your self-confidence deserves such an introduction, as it is the core of who you are. However, it was not an inherited basic characteristic; it was built and sharpened by the environment where you were raised. Unfortunately, whether we spent our formative years in a mansion or in the ghetto, we encountered negative phrases from the mouths of people whom we trust - moms, dads, brothers, sisters, spouses, teachers and friends. If those phrases were repeated consistently we became what those phrases denoted. The subconscious mind does not discriminate the positive from the negative. It just processes the information it receives and replays it throughout our lives, reinforcing those particular phrases.

Suppose your mother repeatedly stated: *"You can't do anything right!"* No matter how intelligent you are, every time you are faced with a decision, great or small, your subconscious mind replays the *"you can't do anything right"* tape, then you procrastinate in making the decision, hence fulfilling the prophecy *"You can't do anything right!"* These old mental tapes, positively or negatively, create our lives. During college I had a friend who upon my first observation seemed to be extremely intelligent, personable and beautiful like a model. As I grew to know this person, I realized she had a low self-esteem. Her father always told her *"You are ugly.", "You are stupid.", "You will never amount to anything."*. Despite the fact, my friend was enrolled in one of the best engineering programs in the country and had a lucrative job promised to her upon graduation, she just could not complete her studies. The old tapes kept replaying, *"You're stupid.",*

Chapter 3

"You will never amount to anything." and hence she fulfilled that prophecy. On the other extreme, she was extremely gifted in crafts, cooking and with children. Compliments in these areas continually came to her. These compliments created a new tape, a positive tape, and a tape that influenced my friend to forsake a lucrative engineering career for a career as a homemaker. Yes, she is the greatest homemaker I have ever seen!

Rewind your mental tapes and replay as many as you can. What did your parents say to you often? Was it positive or negative? Can you recall any that have affected your life? Describe at least three of them here.

_____

_____

_____

_____

_____

Do you fulfill their words? What were they?

_____

_____

_____

_____

Your mental tapes determine how you see yourself and what you believe in. If your mental tapes are positive, you see yourself as confident and hence you see abundance. If your mental tapes are negative, you see yourself negatively, then you see scarcity. Scarcity creates the financial funk, the stress, the fear and the sleepless nights. Scarcity is relative. A millionaire who believes he does not have enough will practice scarcity despite his pile of money. Abundance rests in the universe. All it requires is that you "See it enough to ask for it." When you ask you shall receive it. Abundance is any dream. I always saw myself living in an impeccably decorated house, jet setting on vacations all around the world funded by my business. Ironically, that is the life I lived. But even with a pile of money in the bank I began to fear the effects the recession could have on my financial services firm. Before I knew it, I was in a financial funk. I lived in an affluent neighborhood, driving a luxurious car and living a luxurious lifestyle, but nevertheless, I was in a financial funk.

Still a little skeptical? What tapes are playing today?

_____

_____

_____

_____

_____

Chapter 3

Do they reflect statements made to you during childhood?
_____
_____
_____
_____
_____

Does your current lifestyle reflect the tapes that are playing? Yes or no?

Now that we have addressed your emotional state, let's address your lack of cash issue. Opportunities for more cash abound if you can see them. Unfortunately, most of us can not see them. Those opportunities are internal, within our own minds. Those opportunities are our dreams and passions. Dreams and passions will drive you to work hard and smart. These dreams and passions will cause you to break out of your financial funk. **Let's begin dreaming!**

DREAMS

Imagine this scene: millions of people are drawn to the national jazz legends that perform at the Detroit Jazz Festival. Their works of art are enjoyed by people from all walks of life. At the festival, the environment is carefree and friendly; people act as though the strangers they just met have been their friends for life. Today, a group of strangers *(Bobby Sullivan, Lisa Rogers, John and Mary Smith, William Bennett, and Maria Torres)* are listening to a tribute to Charlie Parker. A discussion surrounding his life and death ensued. A person stated: *"his dreams killed him."* Everyone agrees his dream to become a top paid musician may have killed him. Another stated: "Dreams are hogwash." Another says: "I don't believe in dreams." Someone else said: "Dreams are for babies, grown folks don't dream; we deal with reality."

However, a guy named, Bobby Sullivan, wearing a NASCAR T-shirt, blue jeans and running shoes interjected: *"My dream has been to be a race car driver and have my own pit crew. I have been racing as a semiprofessional. I can't wait to retire to race as a professional driver."* Everyone looked dumbfounded as Bobby spoke. Slowly, one by one they began to admit they each have a secret, deeply buried dream.

Lisa Rogers vehemently stated: *"I hate my job,* what I really love is computers but the schedule is so structured. I would love to work for a contract agency and get some flexibility but the benefits aren't so great". Maria Torres sadly states: "I miss my husband. Her husband died a year ago. They both wanted to sell their house and buy a ranch out West. She has not had the energy to even think about it but she now admits a horse ranch would be a perfect memorial for him.

John and Mary Smith listen intently when John blurts: *"I want to be a beach bum and wear T-shirts/shorts all day."*

Chapter 4

Mary looks blankly at John. He responds by stating: *"I want to live on a houseboat and travel around the world."* His wife states: "We can't live on our boat, it is too small!" John exclaims: *"Let's buy a bigger boat!"*

William Bennett slowly admits he hates his high profile corporate executive job. He would much rather volunteer his time and energy to a children's charity that desires to fight poverty. He wonders out loud to the group if he should retire. Someone states: *"If you can afford to retire, then retire."*

This group of strangers experienced an intense connection as they admitted they all had dreams. Does this scene sound familiar? Sure it does. If we have not had these conversations with others we have had them with ourselves. **The only way to truly get out of your financial funk is to admit you have unfulfilled dreams. The behaviors, the obsessions, the addictions and the trappings of our success come from living a life not true to our dreams.**

Dream, if you dare!

Dream, if you dare! Forget what parents, teachers and other concerned adults told you about dreaming. Dreaming is not a delusionary activity; nor is your head in the clouds or are you slipping away from reality. The truth reveals that reality starts with a dream. William James coined this truth briefly: **"A man may not achieve everything he has dreamed, but he will never achieve anything great without having dreamed it first."** So dream on! Dare to become great! Soar through the future as Orville and Wilber Wright did in their mechanical bird, onto the modern airplane. See the future like Henry Ford, who revolutionized the production of the Horseless Carriage; brighten the future as Thomas Edison who dreamed of a day that electricity could be harnessed to produce an everlasting candle of light. Dream I say if you dare!!! For those skeptical

Dreams

folks, dreams, as defined by Webster's dictionary, are "A fond hope or aspiration – thought imagining as possible-a fanciful vision of the conscious mind."

Reminisce to a time you were approximately 18 years old. Every adult inquisitively asked: "What do you want to be when you finish college?" Can you remember what your answer was? Stop and write it here:

_____

_____

_____

_____

_____

Did you follow this dream passionately through college?
_____

Is your current career an achievement of this dream passion?
_____

    Often you, like me, imagined 3 or more aspirations simultaneously. Every adult, parent, teacher and friend seemed to challenge us to reach for the stars, but no one including our loving parents labeled this activity as dreaming. Well, my friend it is! Instead, we labeled this activity as choosing a career or life inspiration. Aspirations and careers are fancy words for goal-directed passions. Do you stop having goals when you cross the threshold into adulthood? No, it actually begins; for life is a continual process, hence the future is a continual state. I ask you: "What activity excites you to forsake sleep, meals etc.?" Think about it and write it

Chapter 4

here. *(Let go of any inhibitions and let your mind run free as nothing is ridiculous or silly.)*

_____

_____

_____

_____

_____

Are you engaged in this activity either via employment or entrepreneurial venture?

Have you suppressed your passion? _____

Your desires? _____

But your desires could lead you to the position of....

Bill Gates was enrolled in pre-law at Harvard University but his heart was not in his studies. His passion was computers; he just could not get enough of them. Eventually, he and Paul Allen created the first line of programming code, BASIC, for the, Altair 8080, the first micro computer kit. He knew with this first micro computer that Altair invented, the market would explode and every home would soon have a PC. Everyone told him he was crazy. When computers were first invented they cost $600,000+ and literally occupied an entire 2000 square foot room. How could every American afford such a luxury? They could not!!! IBM then approached Bill Gates asking him to write the basic code for their new ROM chips and create an operating system for their computers. He agreed but asked to keep the rights of the DOS operating system that they created. He left Harvard and formed the Microsoft Corporation. Today, 78% of American population use a computer for ordinary tasks and most of those computers run on his software. Could you imagine life without a computer? Personal computers wouldn't be possible without Bill Gate's operating systems that made him the richest man in the world!

As a Man Thinketh

Life's passion can often seem to be impossible and at times unrealistic; however dreams, the first step to reality, awakens you out of sleep. Dreams plant ideas into our brain as if they were seeds. As we focus upon these dreams or ideas, we water them; we nourish them with our thoughts. Before long these ideas become living reality. Things we imagined as impossible become possible!

"As a man thinketh, so is he." Again thoughts and ideas are living things. Whatever you think upon is attracted to you. You think upon riches, riches come to you. You think upon poverty, poverty remains with you. You relish the thought of failure, despite your best efforts, failure will reside with you. But let you, an ordinary person, believe in success and success finds its way to you. For everything you ask for you receive; whatever you seek you shall find; every door you knock upon will be opened. ** But the key is in your brain.

Man only uses a small capacity of his brain, which is the greatest computer drawing board in the world. Your mind produces living thoughts and ideas. The more you focus upon thoughts, the more the creative juices in your

Chapter 4

mind will flow, the more visions you will see. Visions are, foresight, the ability to see into the future and devise wise plans. Visions lay out the road map to the dream.

Madonna, raised in Bay City Michigan, joined a professional ballet troupe. Three weeks on the troupe Madonna confided to her troupe leader that she wanted to become a superstar immediately. Her troupe leader quickly told her it was impossible considering she had just joined the troupe. Madonna quickly resigned from the troupe. While attempting to dance her way to the top she discovered her real talent, singing. She also discovered she liked the street music found in urban America. She had a passion to sing this funky urban street music and even wrote a song. No one took her passion seriously, including famous agents who were known for recognizing talent, until her demo tape excited young party goers at a club. From there, her funky music became the rave, so much so, that in 1983 she recorded *"Like a Virgin"*, a funky urban street song. The song was so popular that she sold 3.5 million copies in 12 weeks. Today, her career has grossed billions of dollars.

Passionate dreams

Do you long to chase your passion? Do you have a secret dream? I dreamed of becoming an entrepreneur. Although I had no money or product to sell, I envisioned myself owning a business and changing people's lives everyday. In 1994 this dream became a reality. I created a company, The Harvard Group Wealth Management LLC, a financial services firm. Little did I know, I would affect people's lives and change them for the better. I then desired to educate the world on how to increase their wealth via home equity and investments. Today my plan is the same, except I am educating the struggling and not the super wealthy. What if I had not forced myself to dream? What if I just continued to work at the career I was extremely talented in, but my heart and my passion belonged somewhere else? If money was plentiful, what lifestyle would you live?

Would you become a:

Traveler/jet setter?
Socialite/volunteer?
Fast paced entrepreneur?
World activist?
Laid-back grandparent?

What would you do?   Detail here:

_____

_____

_____

_____

Chapter 4

Do you have any hobbies that if you had free time they would fill up the time? If yes, List them here:
_____
_____
_____
_____

Are there activities you just ***dreamed*** of doing but could not find time to do? List them here:
_____
_____
_____
_____

What part of your current lifestyle, do you really enjoy? I love having flexibility to travel whenever and wherever I want.
_____
_____
_____
_____

What part of your current lifestyle do you hate?
_____
_____
_____
_____

Dreams

Can you eliminate the part you hate and replace it with parts of your life you love? If so, How would you do that?

_____

_____

_____

What is keeping you from achieving this lifestyle/ career/ job?

_____

_____

_____

Now that you have a general vision of the lifestyle you want to live. Let's explore the options to each lifestyle choice.

_____

_____

_____

_____

Chapter 5

LIFESTYLE OPTIONS

I. Lifestyle exactly the same

There may be several reasons for an individual to stay with his present lifestyle. The most obvious reason is the financial stability your current lifestyle offers. Your current debts and expenditures may use up all of your present income but you have just enough. You may have inadequate personal savings to last the balance of your life. You may have spent your entire life working years to get to your current position and social status. Switching to a new career, company or lifestyle may mean more stress.

Most people are very comfortable, mentally, in their present lifestyle. They know exactly what is expected of them, and have all the skills necessary to perform all the tasks that are required. The satisfaction of a job well done and/or the people we work with may give us the recognition we need for personal satisfaction and high self-esteem. Our co-workers may help to reinforce our personal views and, in reality, may be our best friends.

Keeping your present lifestyle may also deprive you of other rewards. We may not have the time to do all things we would like to do. There may be opportunities that would pay us more for our talents and abilities. Higher levels of growth and satisfaction could be obtained. Reduced physical and emotional stress may be desirable, but not possible, in our present situation.

Lifestyle Options

List the Pros and Cons of Staying in your present lifestyle:

PROS

_____

_____

_____

_____

_____

CONS

_____

_____

_____

_____

Do the Pros out weigh the Cons? If so, how and why?

_____

_____

_____

_____

Let's face it, many people are forced to consider a lifestyle change as mergers, economic downsizing, etc. are forcing people to abandon their careers, houses and other material goods.

Chapter 5

II. Pursue a Hobby in New Job/Career

Do you have a hobby or an activity you love to do which could become a full or part time job? With a pension check available you can move into a job you love to do. Are there any hobbies you could do as employment?

_____

_____

_____

What type of employment could you do?

_____

_____

Bobby Sullivan is an auto mechanic at a Mr. Fix-it shop. He has worked there for 10 years and began working there at age 18. He owned a 5% share in the Mr. Fix-it shop when they were sold to a larger chain. Upon completion of the merger, he was given the option to continue to work for the new company or retire. He is too young to retire. He loves to race. He has always wanted to be full-time, professional race car driver. He has won many races as a part-time, semi-professional. Bobby loves to have a good time and has never worried about the future. He lives a carefree life, despite the fact, he is paying child support for 3 children. Bobby has longed to be a professional race car driver. Will he finally achieve his dream? Do you have a hobby you want to pursue as a career?

Lifestyle Options

III. New Job in the Same Career

Is your area of specialty in hot demand? Can you earn more money in a new job? Is the job contractual, temporary or high risk? Your retirement can serve as a base of stability covering your basic expense.

Lisa Rogers is a 35 year old single parent with 2 children, ages 13 and 15. She wants them to go to college. Her child support payments are not regular. Lisa was an administrative assistant for a computer company in which she earned $2500 a month before she was laid off. She wants to become a computer programmer.

During a job fair she recently discovered she could earn a lot more money working for an agency (approximately $54,000 a year) if she completed her programming classes. She really likes the computer arena. Her company lost a major client and laid her off so she is having a hard time making ends meet. Will she move to the agency?

IV. TURN YOUR HOBBY INTO A BUSINESS!!

Do you have a hobby that could become a successful business? Always wanted to become your "own boss"? Perhaps owning a business can provide the opportunity to do something enjoyable such as: setting desirable work hours or not have to answer to someone else. Starting and running a business is seldom luck. The amount of time, money, stress and physical resources can shut you down in a hurry.

Maria Torres is a 53-year-old financial analyst. Her husband died suddenly a few months ago, leaving her to raise their 15 year old daughter, Carla, alone. He did have $400,000 in life insurance. After graduation, Carla wants to live at home and attend community college. Maria is concerned about making ends meet and wants to go back to the work. She

Chapter 5

loves riding horses. As a matter of fact, she wants to open a riding stable to teach adults to commune with nature. Maria discovered an old ranch in Santa Fe, NM. The ranch would cost $350,000 plus $100,000 to renovate.

The following is a quick review of what it takes to make it work.

Analyze Yourself

The first action you must take is to attempt a thorough investigation of yourself.

1. Are you a passionate person? _____
2. Are you a self-starter? _____
3. Can you accept failure? _____
4. Can you preserve for years until you make a profit? _____
5. Do you enjoy talking to people? _____
6. Can you encourage people to action? _____
7. What experience can you bring to a new business?
   _____
8. Are you a good $money$ manager? _____
9. Are you a good organizer? _____
10. Are you creative? _____
11. Can you solve any problem? _____
12. Have you taken any startup business classes? _____
13. Do you know what it takes to start up a business? _____
14. Do you like marketing/business development? _____

Lifestyle Options

What products or services will you provide?

_____

_____

What are your target markets?

_____

_____

How will you get to your potential customer?

_____

_____

Who is your competition?

_____

_____

What are their strengths?

_____

_____

What are their weaknesses?

_____

_____

Where will you work?

_____

Chapter 5

Will the location matter? Can you work at home?
_____
_____

What type of equipment will you need?
_____
_____

Will you buy used or new?
_____

Will you lease or buy?
_____

How much money can you realistically make?
_____
_____

How much money will you need to get started?
_____

Where will you get it from? A bank or relatives?
_____
_____
_____

Lifestyle Options

Do you have a formal business plan to show a bank? Good credit?

_____

Will you look for alternative ways to finance the venture?

_____

Do you want partners?

_____

Will they be active or passive?

_____

Does the idea of venture capital interest you?

_____

Have you checked government sources?

Have you investigated business start-up assistance programs, such as Bizdom U, Detroit Entrepreneur Institute or Start up Nation?

The biggest determination to the success of a business is the passion of the business owner.

    Howard Schulz is the owner of Starbucks Coffee. Howard propelled Starbucks into a multimillion dollar company. He believed, America would love the Italian experience of dark roasted coffee. The passion propelled the growth of Starbucks; do you have the passion to work to propel your hobby into a profitable business?

Maria Torres has that passion!

Chapter 5

V. LEISURE/JET SET

Many people have worked all their lives and may want to professionally loaf around. They want to do nothing but observe the world around them --- the continents with diverse cultures and exposure to new things. What type of travel do you like? Purely leisure? Educational? Historical? Active/Sport oriented? Or a combination of them all? The question is how to pay the bills for this lifestyle?

Travel has been made cheaper due to internet travel services like www.expedia.com, www.orbitz.com, www.travelocity.com and www.luxurylink.com. These services offer discounts and last minute discount trips. Every transportation entity like trains, planes and buses offer internet discounts. My family of three flew to San Francisco for $191 each and stayed at the Hyatt Regency for $99 dollars a night when the regular rate is $299 per night.

What type of travel are you drawn to?

___

___

John and Mary Smith have been married for over 20 years. John has worked as a millwright for one of the automotive companies for the past 17 years; with overtime he makes $90,000 per year. Mary earns $35,000 as a secretary and has only worked outside the home for the last ten years. They have three children: John Jr. (Buddy), Paul and Anna.

John is planning to retire in 13 years when he qualifies for "30 and out". Unfortunately, he received an early buyout offer yesterday and has 3 children. Anna will graduate from high school in 5 years and would like to go to college. John Jr. is 19 and headed to the Air Force. Paul is 17 and wants to major in business at a major university. After Anna graduates from college, they want to move to North Carolina where they will live on their boat. John wants a yacht. He believes a three bedroom yacht would be more comfortable. It costs $250,000. The Smith's have worked hard all their lives and deserve to live on their yacht but how can they maintain a decent lifestyle when John may be retiring 10 years early and he has little cash saved for retirement?

VI. VOLUNTEER WORK

Today, there are an estimated 175,000 organized volunteer groups, and many are in need of volunteers. Do you have an issue of social cause that drives you? One you could work endlessly to correct? **William Bennett** is 65 years old, and loves helping children. He spent his 28 years as a corporate executive for a Fortune 100 company. He hates his latest assignment. He hangs onto his job because the compensation is fabulous. He spends his free time promoting the cause of charities that benefit children; he is especially sensitive to children in poverty. Upon retirement he plans to become a full time volunteer to assist inner city children. He works for the satisfaction of helping someone else.

Although he has 2 years to retirement where he would receive $15,000 a month he wants to retire now. His expenses total $8000 per month. His pension is $10,000 per month. He has 1.9 million dollars in his corporate savings plan. He wants to leave a gift to one of his charities, approximately $500,000. He works right next to retirees who feel as strong about children as he does. He loves orchestrating fund raisers for his charities.

Although volunteer work does not provide monetary compensation he gets quite excited about helping others.

Chapter 5

He also is able to develop skills he did not have in corporate America. You are thinking this is truly a fictional book as no one lives this way. But, people do in every major city in the world.

Volunteer work can be the best training program ever. Make sure you truly believe in the activity you are volunteering for, so that the work will be satisfying as you build skills to use in the corporate workplace. Ironically, the creation of Hustle & TECHknow Preparatory High School developed from my volunteer work within the Detroit Public Schools. I discovered what can affect test scores, teacher behavior, parent behavior and student behavior.

DREAMING IS ABOUT REALITY

"What you think is real, is your reality", states Robert Kuyosaki in **Retire Young, Retire Rich**! This is the most profound statement I have ever heard. Let me restate it: *"Your Reality is what You Think Is Real."*

This statement means the things; actions and behaviors around you are only as real as you think they are. Your environment manifests your thoughts. My offices are impeccably decorated with upholstered furniture and authentic works of art. My office looks plush because I feel wealthy and desire plush. I could have saved some money and created a cheaper surrounding but I felt wealthy therefore my environment looks wealthy. No matter how much money I had, if I felt poor my surroundings would look poor.

Wayne Dyer's book titled: **"You'll See It When You Believe It"**, sums it up in this manner: "Whatever you focus your thoughts on expands!" If you have a scarcity mentality, it means that we believe in scarcity and that we evaluate our life in terms of its lack. If we dwell on scarcity we are putting energy into what we do not have and this continues to be our experience of life. When you live and breathe prosperity with a belief that every thing is in huge supply and that we are all entitled to have all that we can. You start actively treating yourself and others in this fashion.

Prosperity and abundance is not something that you can manufacture but something that you accept or tune in to. Unlimited prosperity and abundance is all around you. The issue is, Can You See It? The answer is: Only If You Believe It! Life, your environment and your city can be changed by changing your beliefs.

Chapter 6

Belief can be summed up by this poem:

> If you think you are beaten, you are
> If you think you dare not, you don't
> If you like to win, but you think, you can't
> It is almost certain you won't.
>
> If you think you'll lose, you're lost
> For out in the world we find
> Success begins with a fellow's will
> It's all in the state of mind.
>
> If you think you are outclassed, you are,
> You've got to think high to rise
> You've got to be sure of yourself before
> You can ever win a prize.
>
> "Life's battles don't always go
> To the stronger or faster man,
> But soon or late the man who wins
> Is the man **WHO THINKS HE CAN!**"

Bobby Sullivan understood this poem. He dreamed of being a professional race car driver. Little did he know his confidence in his dream would spark others to dream. It did as Bobby had faith in his dream.

Here are four steps in changing your beliefs to create a positive and abundant dream reality:

How to Attract Money

Robert Griswold in **"How to Attract Money"** defines the four steps as:

1. You make assumptions. Most limitations are a result of negative programming of your childhood. Such phrases as "We will never be rich." "We cannot live rich." "We have struggled for 50 generations." "We have always lived in a rented home." "We have always lived in the projects." "We have never had enough to eat." "No one had every graduated from high school in our family." "No one in this family will ever go to college."

2. Your behavior is a result of your beliefs about yourself.

3. Your behavior encourages certain beliefs.

4. Your behavior changes as a result of your assumptions.

Your belief becomes a reality for you. You know the belief you have accepted as so.

Unfortunately most reality is negative and limited. The question "is your life the reality you dreamed of?" If not, you can reverse that programming.

Chapter 6

Six steps to Dream Programming:

1. Recognize your negative programming. Write down negative comments that you live by.
   _____
   _____
   _____
   _____
   _____

2. Review comments. Who said them to you?
   _____
   _____
   _____
   _____

3. Are they really true? Or did you make them come true?
   _____
   _____

4. Neutralize the negative statements and replace them with positive statements.
   _____
   _____
   _____

Sample Affirmations
- I choose to be wealthy.
- Financial independence is mine.
- Money is my friend.
- I am comfortable having money.
- Large amounts of money are coming to me.
- Money flows to me easily and naturally.
- The more money I have, the more I can live my dream.
- My dream is _____.
- I will generate _____ income this year.
- Everyday I am moving closer to my dream.
- I am a money magnet!

5. Make the positive statement into an assumption.

Write your affirmations on an index card. Review your affirmations first thing in the morning and before you fall asleep. An ideal place for them is the bathroom or bedroom mirror, or the refrigerator so that they are in plain sight.

6. Your behavior changes as a result of your positive assumptions. Your new belief.
   - Positive assumptions move you to action.
   - Establish daily action plans to dream

Suppose you have difficulty saving, as you like spending money. If you spend $10 dollars a day on lottery tickets, commit to saving $5 dollars per day. That small change is $150 per month, $1800 per year, and $18,000 per decade.

Belief causes a person to act, their actions create the situation, hence, belief creates reality. Modern Psychology states, "It's takes 21 days to establish a new habit." Follow your new habit for at least 21 days straight.

Your positive belief now becomes a reality!

Chapter 6

What is your belief?

My belief has always been that I will become wealthy even while sitting in a HUD project in Flint, MI. I believed I was wealthy. In high school when everyone worked a minimum wage job at the local fast food restaurant, I worked at the library as a page. I loved and still love to read. My passion for books allowed me to earn 1½ times minimum wage. My grades were excellent so I was awarded a college scholarship to the University of Michigan. While the scholarship paid for tuition and my room and board, I was forced to work to achieve my goal of acquiring $10,000 upon graduation from college. Every job I received, I earned at least twice the minimum wage. My belief was that I deserved better than average and that is what I got. Rich thoughts drew me to rich experienced jobs. Opportunities after college seemed to abound as I only saw opportunity.

But as easily as opportunities came, they went, when I married a man who believed in scarcity. No matter what opportunities were available, he saw lack, scarcity and poverty. Despite our six-figure family income, we struggled for nine years because his thoughts of scarcity and poverty were dominant.

When I divorced him and negative thoughts left, my opportunities began to rebound. WHY? The universe contains both abundance and scarcity, rich and poor, good and bad; but it's up to us to choose!

Dreams are reality and your reality is based on your thoughts. Thoughts are thriving things, which become the basis of your dreams. Today, my dream is to retire at age 50, in year 2017 to a tropical island in the Caribbean, where I can write best-sellers, that will encourage millions of people worldwide to grow and expand their wealth consciousness. I expect a multimillionaire net worth to live off. For most people, that dream seems rushed and absurd. However, that dream began in 1994, fourteen years ago. This book is a part of that dream.

Dreaming Is About Reality

Bobby Sullivan realized the racing industry was a tight group and began to move into the industry, first as a volunteer pit crew member and then as a paid pit crew member. He graduated to semi-professional driver two years ago. He expects to become a paid, professional driver.

Lisa Rogers wants to go work for a contract agency as a computer programmer. She expects she will work until age 62, when she qualifies for Social Security. After much searching, she found one contract agency who has a major project for her to work on, if she goes back to school and get her programming credentials. They offered her an hourly rate of $20 or $41,600 annually. She will be able to invest $10,000 annually to save towards her retirement; she wants to move to Brazil.

Maria Torres, plans to buy that ranch in Santa Fe and revive it. Her job gives 9 weeks of vacation and 3 weeks of personal time in which she plans on using to begin working on the riding stable and will complete it when she retires in 2 years.

John and Mary Smith can't wait to retire as John has worked 65 hours a week for the past 17 years. They just want to relax on their boat. John found a new job in North Carolina. He bought a smaller house and a small yacht. They have done upgrades to the house and plan to sell it when John retires.

William Bennett has spent 28 years as a volunteer and activist, assisting children's organizations. He has chaired fund-raising committees and executive boards, so he fully understands a nonprofit organization. He is known as "A children's friend and community activist." He can not wait to work as a full-time volunteer. Last week, he was at a party when the chairman of a local charity asked him to interview for their president's position. He is elated to have the opportunity to lead a charity whose mission is to house and rehabilitate wayward youth.

Chapter 6

Are you making steps to achieve your dream reality? What are those steps? Detail them here.

_____
_____
_____
_____
_____
_____
_____
_____

What steps do you need to make in the short term?

_____
_____
_____
_____
_____
_____
_____
_____

Dreaming Is About Reality

These steps are beginning of your plan to achieve your dream. Yes, I said "Plan." It has been documented that three percent of the U.S. population has a written plan. This three percent usually completes their plans. They avoid financial funk altogether. To break out of your financial funk, you must determine where you want to go. You must write that plan down. Spend some time deciding where you want go. Write 101 goals you desire to happen in your life.

101 Goals

1. _____   2. _____
3. _____   4. _____
5. _____   6. _____
7. _____   8. _____
9. _____   10. _____
11. _____   12. _____
13. _____   14. _____
15. _____   16. _____
17. _____   18. _____
19. _____   20. _____
21. _____   22. _____
23. _____   24. _____
25. _____   26. _____
27. _____   28. _____
29. _____   30. _____
31. _____   32. _____
33. _____   34. _____
35. _____   36. _____
37. _____   38. _____
39. _____   40. _____
41. _____   42. _____

Chapter 6

43. _____ 44. _____
45. _____ 46. _____
47. _____ 48. _____
49. _____ 50. _____
51. _____ 52. _____
53. _____ 54. _____
55. _____ 56. _____
57. _____ 58. _____
59. _____ 60. _____
61. _____ 62. _____
63. _____ 64. _____
65. _____ 66. _____
67. _____ 68. _____
69. _____ 70. _____
71. _____ 72. _____
73. _____ 74. _____
75. _____ 76. _____
77. _____ 78. _____
79. _____ 80. _____
81. _____ 82. _____
83. _____ 84. _____
85. _____ 86. _____
87. _____ 88. _____
89. _____ 90. _____
91. _____ 92. _____
93. _____ 94. _____
95. _____ 96. _____
97. _____ 98. _____
99. _____ 100. _____
101. _____

Dreaming Is About Reality

You are probably thinking: *"It is hard to plan or think about wealth when we are struggling to eat, live or find a job."* Yes, it is. Positive thinking will not change your life in an instant. Positive thinking changes how you see your life now.

For a period of my life, I ate ramen noodles or rice and no meat at least 4 days a week. I went to the dollar store and bought nice plates, and water goblets. I sat the table every day like I was eating Filet Mignon. I said my blessing and gratefully ate those ramen noodles. If the plate or glass broke, I did not get upset. It cost a dollar. Eventually, I added canned meat to the noodles. Next, I was cooking fresh meat. The progression from meatless meals to fresh meat happened without a clear changing point. All I remember is repeating my affirmations often, even in the blessing of the food.

Live wealthy, as if you are already rich. You may not be able to go on shopping sprees or buy new cars/clothes, but you can decorate your house as if it is a mansion, albeit frugally. Positive thoughts drive away poverty and scarcity as you, the individual refuses to accept them. One year, I decorated my entire Christmas tree from ornaments purchased at Dollar Tree. People who visited my house thought that I spent a lot of money on the tree. Because I studied the look and feel of an expensive ornament, I knew how to purchase a similar ornament at a fraction of the cost. I looked at lots of home magazines standing in the magazine rack of Border's bookstore. I surfed the internet learning from Martha Stewart and B. Smith. I read etiquette books, wealthy living guides, especially Forbes magazine. I learned everything about the wealthy, how they live and how they got wealthy. I learned to live wealthy long before I became wealthy.

You must create your riches within your mind first, before they ever become real. You must spend time in silence to hear the infinite opportunities and ideas blow your way.

Chapter 6

It only takes one idea to become wealthy. For some of the wealthy people on Forbes 400, it was French fries, tires or candy bars. It was one idea. What is going to be your idea to break out of your financial funk? Tax Preparation? Answering phone calls for companies like Arise? Modeling? Day care? Foster care? What is it going to be?

Sit in silence with your eyes closed. No music, television, no sound for 15 minutes. What comes to mind. Write it down here. Sit for 15 minutes in silence every day for the next 30 days and to write down more ideas.

Day 1
_____
_____
_____
_____
_____

Day 2
_____
_____
_____
_____

Day 3
_____
_____
_____
_____
_____

Dreaming Is About Reality

Day 4

Day 5

Day 6

Day 7

Day 8

Chapter 6

Day 9

Day 10

Day 11

Day 12

Day 13

Dreaming Is About Reality

Day 14

Day 15

Day 16

Day 17

Day 18

Chapter 6

Day 19

Day 20

Day 21

Day 22

Day 23

Dreaming Is About Reality

Day 24

Day 25

Day 26

Day 27

Day 28

Chapter 6

Day 29
_____
_____
_____
_____

Day 30
_____
_____
_____
_____

Did any good ideas come to mind? A good idea satisfies the need of a group of people. It could be extremely absurd or conservative. It does not matter. If it satisfies a need, people will buy it, use it or trade it. It could be simple, like a professional sounding voice or as complicated as Google. If you chased away negative thoughts during your 15 minutes, the Universe who... is God, will bring wonderful ideas to break you out of your financial funk. This book is one of those ideas to assist me.

BIBLIOGRAPHY

Allen, James, **As a Man Thinketh**, 1902 Public Domain,
Byrne, Rhonda, **The Secret**, Atria Books/Beyond Words 2006

Canfield, Jack, **The Success Principles How to Get from Where you are to Where you Want to Be**, Collins, 2006

Dyer, Wayne, **The Power of Intention**, Carlsbad, CA; Hay House, 2004

Dyer, Wayne, **10 Secrets for Success and Inner Peace**, Carlsbad, CA; Hay House, 2001

Dyer, Wayne, **You'll See It When You Believe It: The Way to Your Personal Transformation**, New York, NY, Harper Collins, 1989

Griswold, Robert, **How to Attract Money**, New York, NY Warner Bros. 1993

Jack Canfield, Hansen, Mark Victor, **The Power of Focus**, Deerfield Beach, Health Communications, 2000

Hill, Napoleon, **Think and Grow Rich**, Filiquarian Publishing, 2005

Kimbro, Dennis, **What Makes the Great Great**, New York, New York, Doubleday, 1998

Kuyosaki, Robert, **Retire Young, Retire Rich**!

Labiers, Douglas, **Modern Madness: the Emotional Fallout of Success**, 1986

Robbins, Tony, Unlimited Power: **The New Science of Achievement**, Robbins Research Institute, 1986

Williamson, Marianne, **A Return to Love: Reflections on the Principles of "A Course in Miracles"**, New York, New York Harper Collins 1992

ABOUT THE AUTHOR

Ida Byrd-Hill is the President of Uplift, Inc., a 501(c)3 an Idea Incubator whose mission is reconstructing communities, one idea at a time, utilizing property (intellectual, real estate and technology) to lift individuals from tragedy. Her latest project was Hustle & TECHknow Preparatory High School, a cyber school for juvenile delinquents and dropouts. Prior to this project she spent 10 years as a financial advisor/ mortgage loan officer having advised 2200 individual clients and 10 corporate clients. She also worked 5 years in human resources and executive search. She is the proud parent of teenage twins, Kevin and Karen Hill.

She can be reached at BreakinOut@upliftinc.org

Appendix

Speaking Inquiry
Bring the Power of "Breakin' Out" to Your Organization!

Ida Byrd-Hill has a message of success for your audience, as well as an engaging style that will make your entire organization shift into high-gear, both personally and professionally!

For more than 20 years, Ida Byrd-Hill has studied the elements of what makes successful people successful. She knows what motivates them, what drives them, and what inspires them... and she brings this critical insight to your organization.

Ida has created the definitive method to help people create breakthrough results in everything they do. She will push them to achieve greater results in their personal life and hence improve their professional life.

Whether you hire Ida for 1 hour, or 1 day, here are just a few of the strategies you can expect your audience to learn...

- **DEVELOP** tools to shape perspectives and solve problems
- **TRANSITION** from where you are to where you want to be
- **FOCUS** using techniques to achieve goals and objectives
- **SHIFT** attitude beliefs from the "I can't" to "I can" solution models
- **VISUALIZE** using specific techniques to achieve desired outcomes
- **MASTER** key disciplines of finances and entrepreneurial spirit

If your organization can benefit from Ida Byrd-Hill and her Breakin' Out of your Financial Funk message, contact her at BreakinOut@upliftinc.org.

Chapter 7

Share This Book With Others!

Please make checks payable to:
"Breakin' Out of Financial Funk!!!"

To pay by money order, check or credit card;
please return this form to:
Breakin' Out of Financial Funk!!!
P.O. Box 241488
Detroit, MI 48224

Name: _____
Address: _____
City: _____ State: _____ Zip: _____
Phone: _____ Fax: _____
Email: _____

For Credit Card Orders   ☐ Visa   ☐ MasterCard
#: _____ - _____ - _____ - _____
Exp. Date: _____ / _____

Quantity of books:
_____ $16.95 Per Book

Shipping & Handling:

1 book	2-3	4-5	6-7	8-10
$4.50	$10.50	$12.00	$15.00	$20.00

Amount

$ _____ "Shipping Total"

$ _____ Total Amount

For discounts on large quantity orders or more information call:
email:
BreakinOut@upliftinc.org

Books can also be ordered online at the Lulu.com, Amazon.com, Borders.com, Barnesandnoble.com and other internet retailers. For those who order the book directly from the author at www.upliftinc.org you will receive a special surprise from the author.

Appendix

Share your Stories

Did completing the assignments in this book cause you to reflect on some interesting stories?

Did you have fun Breakin' Out of Your Financial Funk?

If so, please provide us with your stories. Please send them by electronic mail to:
BreakinOut@upliftinc.org
Or to:
Ida Byrd-Hill
Breakin' Out of Your Financial Funk!!!
P.O. Box 241488
Detroit, MI 48224

Please note stories, pictures etc. become the property of Upheaval Media and will not be returned unless sent with a self-addressed, stamped envelope.

www.ingramcontent.com/pod-product-compliance
Lightning Source LLC
Chambersburg PA
CBHW021025090426
42738CB00007B/914